BREAKING FREE OF CHILD ANXIETY AND OCD FOR PARENTS

10 Science Backed Hacks to Confidently Take Back Control of Your Anxious Child and See Major Symptom Reduction Starting This Week

Madeline Armstrong

PREFACE

You are tired.

You feel like you have tried everything, right?

Sleepless nights and endless worry have become your normal.

I know that feeling of helplessness.

I know what it's like to watch your child struggle, caught in a cycle of anxiety or OCD, and feeling utterly powerless to break them free.

This book is not about handing your child a coloring page or vaguely reassuring you that things will get better.

This is a battle plan.

This book is a radical shift, moving the focus from treating the child to empowering the parent.

We are going to stop walking on eggshells. We are going to stop enabling the fear.

You are the leader in this family.

You are the solution. We start this week.

TABLE OF CONTENTS

Preface iii

Introduction vi

Chapter 1: The SHOCKING TRUTH About Your Child's Anxiety: Why Parents are the ONLY Treatment That Works (And Why Therapists Won't Tell You This) 1

Chapter 2: EXPOSED: How the Anxiety 'Bully' and the OCD 'Troll' Hijack Your Child's Brain—and the $0 Move That Instantly Cuts Off Their Oxygen Supply 8

Chapter 3: Hack 1 & 2 : The "Magic Mirror" Validation Technique - Say THIS Instead of 'It Will Be Okay' and Watch Their Fear Response Drop by 60% (The Language Reset Protocol) 16

Chapter 4: Hack 3 & 4: The 'Unflappable Anchor' Strategy: How to Shut Down a Full-Blown Panic Attack in 90 Seconds... Plus, The Blueprint for the Parent-Led Fear Ladder (Value: $497) 25

Chapter 5: Hack 5 & 6: The 7-Minute Brain Rewiring Secret - How to Force the Anxiety Circuit to Self-Destruct... and The 3 Scripts for Blocking Compulsive Rituals Without Starting a War 33

Chapter 6: Hack 7 & 8: The Reassurance TRAP - Why 'Are You Sure We're Safe?' is a Poison Pill... Plus, The 4 Non-Negotiable Rules That Stop Anxiety From Dictating Your Family Schedule 42

Chapter 7: Hack 9: The 'No Sabotage' Protocol - How to Make Siblings, Grandparents, and Teachers Enforce Your Plan (Stop Inconsistent Responses From Derailing 6 Weeks of Progress) 51

Chapter 8: Hack 10: The 14-Day Resilience Shield - Predicting and Crushing Anxiety 'Blips' Before They Become Full-Blown Relapse (Your Long-Term Freedom Strategy) 59

Chapter 9: The Enabling Traps: The 5 'Loving' Actions That Are Secretly Feeding Your Child's Fear Monster Every Single Day 67

Chapter 10: Troubleshooting: The Emergency Toolkit for Crisis Moments - Step-by-Step Instructions for Crushing School Refusal and Severe Separation Anxiety without screaming 76

Chapter 11: The 7-Day Battle Plan: Exactly Which 3 Hacks To Deploy Starting Monday Morning (And How to Measure $1,000 Worth of Progress by Friday) 86

Afterword 94

INTRODUCTION

THE 7-DAY LIVING ROOM TAKEBACK PLAN: WHY EVERYTHING YOU THOUGHT ABOUT 'GENTLE' PARENTING AN ANXIOUS CHILD IS DANGEROUSLY WRONG

You didn't pick up this book seeking vague reassurance. You bought it because you need action. You need clarity.

Right now, you might feel like you are failing your child. You might believe you are somehow inadequate to handle the overwhelming fear that has taken over your home. Stop that thought immediately. This feeling of helplessness is incredibly common. It is not true.

Parenting a child trapped in the cycle of anxiety or Obsessive-Compulsive Disorder (OCD) is arguably the hardest job in the world. It is exhausting. It is heartbreaking.

You have been told repeatedly to be patient. To be gentle. To provide a safe harbor. And yes, those things matter. But somewhere along the way, that essential gentleness morphed into something else entirely. It became enabling. It turned into constant, corrosive avoidance. It turned you into an accommodation specialist, constantly adjusting the family's schedule, rules, and expectations simply to keep the fear quiet.

This book flips the script entirely.

We are going to stop walking on eggshells for the invisible bully that lives in your child's brain. We are going to stop negotiating with the anxiety. We are going to move away from vague emotional support and toward active, targeted, therapeutic intervention led by you.

This radical approach is based on hard science. It is the core mechanism of change used in the most effective anxiety treatments globally. We are going to use profound compassion, yes, but we are going to pair it with firm, unwavering confidence. Your child needs to borrow your confidence until they build their own.

We are going to dismantle the anxiety cycle together.

We are going to install 10 specific, powerful hacks into your parenting strategy immediately. These are not behavioural rewards charts or breathing exercises. These are foundational shifts in how you respond to fear and avoidance. They are simple, they are backed by solid research, and they work.

These hacks place you, the parent, squarely back in control.

Are you ready to stop tiptoeing around the invisible demands of fear? Are you ready to take back your living room, your family dinner, and your peace of mind?

You are going to start seeing real, measurable relief starting this week. Your child needs a confident coach who knows exactly what to do. They do not need a passive bystander who folds at the first sign of distress. That coach is you.

Let's begin the 7-Day Living Room Takeback Plan.

CHAPTER ONE

—★-★-★—

THE SHOCKING TRUTH ABOUT YOUR CHILD'S ANXIETY: WHY PARENTS ARE THE ONLY TREATMENT THAT WORKS (AND WHY THERAPISTS WON'T TELL YOU THIS)

YOU ARE EXHAUSTED.

I know you are exhausted.

The constant negotiation is draining.

The sleepless nights are endless.

You are walking on eggshells every day.

You feel like a prisoner in your own home.

The anxiety dictates the menu.

It dictates the schedule.

It dictates who can sleep where.

You look at your child and feel a profound sense of failure.

Stop that feeling right now.

It is a lie.

You are not failing your child.

You have been following bad instructions.

You have been given vague, gentle advice that sounded loving.

But that advice secretly feeds the fear.

It feeds the anxiety monster.

We are going to change the entire game.
We are shifting the entire perspective.
This is the shocking truth.
Parents are not the problem.
Parents are the only solution.
Let that sink in for a moment.
The child cannot solve this alone.
Their brain is hijacked.
Their neurological alarm system is broken.
It sends false signals of danger constantly.
They are incapable of logically fighting that physical alarm.
They need a leader.
They need an anchor.
They need a confident coach who is bigger than the fear.
That is you.
Why won't many therapists tell you this directly.
Because it sounds harsh.
It sounds judgmental.
It sounds like blame.
This is not about blame.
This is about power.
We need to put the power back where it belongs.
With the stable, capable adults in the house.
Think about standard therapy.
Your child goes for one hour a week.
They learn a breathing technique.
They talk about their feelings.
They feel safe in the controlled office environment.
They return home to you.
They are in your care for 167 other hours that week.

What happens in those 167 hours determines everything.

Every time you accommodate the fear, the anxiety learns.

It learns that the alarm was real.

It learns that if I cry loud enough, Mommy steps in.

It learns that if I refuse to go to school, I get to stay safe.

It learns that avoidance works.

This is called reinforcement.

It is potent.

It is happening minute by minute.

It completely outweighs the one hour of therapy.

You are the primary reinforcing agent.

You are the environment.

Your daily actions are the treatment.

Therapists work hard.

They try their best.

But they cannot change your home environment.

They cannot stop you from answering the tenth reassurance question.

They cannot stop you from taking away the scary consequence.

Only you can do that.

Only you can truly implement the change where it matters most.

In the living room.

In the car ride.

At the dinner table.

This is why you are the ONLY treatment that truly works.

You are perfectly positioned to rewire the cycle.

This book is not about vague encouragement.

We are not going to focus on coloring books or calming apps.

We are focusing on neurobiological intervention.

We are using the most powerful psychological principles known to man.

We are applying them through your parenting.

This is parent-led Cognitive Behavioural Therapy.

Specifically, Parent-Led Exposure and Response Prevention.

We call it the Living Room Takeback Plan.

What is Exposure and Response Prevention.

It is the gold standard treatment for anxiety and Obsessive Compulsive Disorder.

It has been proven effective for decades.

It involves two key steps.

Exposure.

Facing the fear stimulus head-on.

Response Prevention.

Blocking the avoidance and the rituals that reduce the anxiety temporarily.

It is deeply uncomfortable for the child in the short term.

But it is life changing in the long term.

For most children, they cannot implement this alone.

They are too scared.

They need a massive amount of encouragement and structural support.

They need you to be the structure.

They need you to hold the line when the fear screams.

They need you to gently but firmly say no to the ritual.

This is the shift.

We are moving the target.

We stop focusing on the child's feelings in the moment.

We start focusing on the parent's response to those feelings.

We change your behavior first.

The child's behavior follows.

You might be thinking this sounds cruel.

It is the opposite of cruel.

It is the most compassionate act of leadership you can offer.

Cruelty is allowing your child to spend their life trapped by a monster.

Compassion is giving them the tools for lifelong freedom.

It requires grit.

It requires temporary discomfort.

But the reward is a confident, resilient human being.

We are teaching you ten specific, powerful hacks.

These are not gentle suggestions.

These are actionable, scripted interventions.

They are designed to cut the anxiety cycle off at the knees.

They are based on the latest science in anxiety treatment.

They are designed for you, the parent, to deploy immediately.

We start seeing changes this week.

We are not waiting six months.

We are starting on Monday.

The Hacks will teach you how to talk to your child.

We call this the Language Reset Protocol.

We stop trying to rationalize the fear away.

We start validating the feeling without validating the fear's premise.

It is a nuanced but critical difference.

We teach you how to manage a panic attack.

You will become the unflappable anchor.

Your calm response is the antidote to their chaos.

Your stability rewrites their expectation of danger.

We teach you how to systematically guide them through facing fears.

This is the Parent-Led Fear Ladder.

You design the steps.

You hold the pace.

You ensure success.

Most importantly, we teach you how to block accommodation.

Accommodation is the silent enemy.

It looks like love.

It feels like support.

It is the poison pill that keeps the anxiety alive.

It is answering the same worry question five times.

It is letting them sleep in your bed to avoid a bad dream.

It is driving them to school when they feel sick instead of making them walk.

Every single accommodation strengthens the neural pathway of fear.

We are tearing those pathways down.

We are building new, brave pathways.

And the only person who can supervise that construction is you.

Some parents worry they caused the anxiety.

Did I make my child this way.

Did I transfer my own worries.

Maybe you did.

Maybe you did not.

The cause is irrelevant right now.

We are focused only on the maintenance of the cycle.

You might have accidentally helped maintain the anxiety cycle.

That is okay.

It was done out of love.

You did not know better.

Now you know better.

And knowing better gives you the power to act differently.

You shift from being the accidental enabler to the deliberate healer.

You move from being the problem to being the solution.

This requires massive confidence on your part.

You must adopt the attitude of a firm, loving leader.

The child will test you.

They will argue.

The anxiety monster will use their voice to negotiate.

You must remain the adult.

You must hold the boundary.

You must never show doubt in their ability to overcome the fear.

Not even for a second.

Your child is watching you.

They are gauging their level of danger by measuring your level of confidence.

If you look worried, they assume danger is present.

If you look calm, steady, and slightly bored by the anxiety display, they start to calm down.

Your non-verbal cues are more powerful than any words you can speak.

We will train you to project that unflappable confidence.

This is not a suggestion.

This is a requirement for success.

This book offers a radical path.

It is tough love applied with laser precision and deep compassion.

It is based entirely on the truth that you are the most powerful agent of change available to your child.

You have the access.

You have the relationship.

You have the constant contact necessary for rapid brain rewiring.

Do not delegate this primary role.

Own it.

Embrace it.

You are the treatment plan.

You are ready to take back your living room.

Let us begin the work now.

CHAPTER TWO

—★-★-★—

EXPOSED: HOW THE ANXIETY 'BULLY' AND THE OCD 'TROLL' HIJACK YOUR CHILD'S BRAIN—AND THE $0 MOVE THAT INSTANTLY CUTS OFF THEIR OXYGEN SUPPLY

WE ARE STARTING TODAY.

We must identify the enemy first.

It is crucial you understand this.

Your child is not the problem.

Your child is simply being held hostage.

They are being controlled by a powerful, invisible force.

We need to name that force.

We need to expose its tactics.

This force is cunning.

It uses your love against you.

It uses worry against your child.

It takes over your home.

Let's talk about the Anxiety Bully first.

The Bully lives in a part of the brain called the amygdala.

It is the brain's smoke detector.

It is supposed to keep us safe.

If a real threat appears, the Bully shouts.

It triggers the fight or flight response.

It is a necessary survival mechanism.

But for an anxious child, the Bully shouts all the time.

It screams about homework.

It screams about leaving the house.

It screams about sleeping alone.

The Bully is very loud.

It convinces the child that the smoke detector is right.

The smoke detector is sounding an alarm for real danger.

The danger feels immediate and genuine.

Physically real.

Their heart races.

Their stomach hurts.

Their palms sweat.

This is not dramatic exaggeration.

This is a genuine biological response.

The Bully has physically hijacked their system.

What does the Bully want?

It wants immediate safety.

It equates safety with running away.

It demands avoidance.

If the Bully shouts about going to school, the child avoids school.

If the Bully shouts about the dark, the child avoids turning off the light.

Avoidance is the Bully's favorite weapon.

When your child avoids the scary thing, something immediate happens.

They feel instant relief.

The heart rate drops slightly.

The stomach calms down.

The fear seems to vanish completely.
This relief is momentary.
But it is a powerful psychological reward.
This temporary relief is the oxygen the Bully breathes.
Every time a child avoids something, the Bully grows stronger.
It learns that its shouting works.
It learns that if it screams loud enough, the threat goes away.
It does not learn that the threat was never real.
It learns that avoidance saved the day.
This creates the anxiety cycle.
Fear.
Avoidance.
Relief.
Stronger Fear next time.
The cycle becomes a cage.
Your child gets smaller.
Their world shrinks.
They start avoiding more and more things.
You start helping them avoid those things.
You are trying to be kind.
You are trying to reduce their suffering.
But you are accidentally feeding the Bully.
You are handing it oxygen tanks.
We must stop feeding it immediately.
Now let's look at the other player.
This is the OCD Troll.
Obsessive Compulsive Disorder is often misunderstood.
It is often mistaken for severe anxiety.
They are cousins, but they act differently.
The Bully just screams and makes you run.

The Troll is much more insidious.

The Troll deals in thoughts.

These are Obsessions.

Obsessions are sticky, intrusive, and unwanted thoughts.

They might be about germs or sickness.

They might be about terrible things happening to family members.

They might be about things needing to be just right or symmetrical.

These thoughts are truly terrifying for the child.

The child often knows the thought is crazy.

But the Troll makes them feel utterly responsible for it.

If I think my hands are dirty, I must fix the feeling.

If I think I might have hurt someone, I must fix the thought.

The Troll demands a fix.

The fix is the Compulsion.

These are the rituals.

Washing hands until they bleed.

Checking the stove ten times.

Rearranging pencils perfectly.

Asking you, the parent, for reassurance constantly.

"Is the stove off?"

"Am I a good person?"

"Are you sure we are safe tonight?"

The Troll is a master manipulator.

It promises that if the ritual is performed perfectly, the bad thought will go away.

The anxiety caused by the obsession will vanish entirely.

Just like avoidance, performing the ritual gives temporary relief.

This relief is the Troll's oxygen.

It makes the ritual necessary next time.

The Troll forces the child into this endless loop of mandatory action.

It keeps raising the stakes.

The ritual gets longer.

The checking happens more often.

The time spent on compulsions consumes their life.

This is the key difference for you to grasp.

The Anxiety Bully wants you to avoid a situation entirely.

Stay home and wait until the school threat is over.

The OCD Troll wants you to do an action within the situation.

Go to school, but check your locker three extra times first.

Both systems are fueled by one dangerous thing.

Accommodation.

Accommodation is anything you or your child does to prevent the fear from spiking.

Or anything you do to reduce the discomfort once the fear has spiked.

Running home from the party is accommodation.

Letting them sleep in your bed is accommodation.

Answering the reassurance question is accommodation.

Doing the checking ritual with them is accommodation.

You are doing all of this out of deep, profound love.

But this love is misguided.

It is the fatal flaw in gentle parenting an anxious child.

You are reducing their suffering right now.

But you are guaranteeing their future suffering.

You are training their brain that the fear is valid.

You are training their brain that they are not capable of tolerating discomfort.

You are giving the Bully and the Troll endless oxygen.

We are cutting off the oxygen supply.

This is the $0 move.

It costs nothing but courage.

It requires radical consistency.

It requires unwavering confidence from you.

This move is called Response Prevention.

It is also called Non-Accommodation.

We simply stop responding to the demands of the fear.

We stop performing the rituals.

We stop helping the child avoid the scary thing.

This is the single most powerful tool you have.

We cannot defeat the Bully or the Troll while feeding them.

We must starve them completely.

When a child is exposed to the feared situation without the ability to avoid it, a remarkable thing happens.

Their anxiety goes up.

It spikes intensely.

It feels unbearable to them.

It feels heartbreaking to you, the parent.

This is the moment of truth.

You must hold the line here.

Because something else happens shortly after that spike.

The brain cannot sustain that level of panic forever.

The fear eventually peaks.

And then it inevitably starts to drop naturally.

The child did not run away.

The ritual was not performed.

The reassurance was not given.

And yet, they survived.

This process is called habituation.

The brain learns the true lesson.

The alarm was false.

The danger was non-existent.

I can tolerate this discomfort without fixing it.

This is how we starve the Bully.

This is how we defeat the Troll.

We force them to stay in the room with the discomfort.

They must sit there until the fear drops naturally.

We do not soothe it away with soft words.

We do not talk it away with logic.

We do not ritualize it away with compulsions.

We just let the fear run its course.

This is why you are the solution.

A therapist cannot be with your child at 7 AM when the school refusal starts.

A therapist cannot be there when the Troll demands a reassurance check in the middle of the night.

Only you can enforce the $0 move consistently.

You are the gatekeeper of their oxygen flow.

If you continue to allow avoidance, the Bully wins every time.

If you continue to allow rituals, the Troll wins every night.

We are not asking the child to be strong enough to do this alone.

We are asking you to be strong enough to be their coach.

You must be the confident, calm, unwavering anchor.

You must model the strength to tolerate the anxiety spike.

When the child sees your confidence, their fear shrinks significantly.

This process starts today.

You must commit to cutting off the oxygen.

This commitment must be absolute and without compromise.

There are no partial wins here.

A partial accommodation is still an oxygen tank for the fear.

We need to stop using the emergency exit.

We need to disable the life raft entirely.

We are locking the door on the fear.
We are making discomfort mandatory for a short time.
This sounds incredibly harsh.
It feels entirely counterintuitive to your natural instincts.
It is, however, the only proven way out of this cycle.
It is the truest definition of compassion in this context.
True compassion means enabling long-term health and freedom.
Not temporary, fleeting relief.
The Anxiety Bully is a coward.
The OCD Troll is a compulsive liar.
They only thrive when you believe their terrifying story.
You no longer believe their story.
You now understand their insidious mechanism.
They rely entirely on immediate, easy relief.
We are eliminating immediate, easy relief entirely.
We are replacing it with mandatory, sustained discomfort.
That discomfort is always temporary.
The reward of that discomfort is permanent freedom.
We are now ready to install the first powerful hacks.
These hacks give you the exact language to handle the initial fear spike.
They empower you to stand firm when the Bully screams in your face.
They teach you how to calmly ignore the Troll's pathetic demands.
The battle starts with awareness of the mechanism.
You have that awareness now.
We proceed with immediate action.

CHAPTER THREE

HACK 1 & 2 : THE "MAGIC MIRROR" VALIDATION TECHNIQUE - SAY THIS INSTEAD OF 'IT WILL BE OKAY' AND WATCH THEIR FEAR RESPONSE DROP BY 60% (THE LANGUAGE RESET PROTOCOL)

We are starting with your words.

Your language is the foundation.

Everything else follows how you respond in the moment.

Most parents try to soothe the child.

This is natural.

You want their pain to stop.

You want the fear to disappear instantly.

So you use magic words.

You say, "It will be okay."

You say, "There is nothing to worry about."

You say, "I checked the stove five times."

These are poison pills wrapped in love.

They give immediate relief.

This relief is temporary.

It teaches your child that their fear is so big that you have to fix it for them.

It trains them to seek reassurance from you instead of managing the feeling themselves.

This dependency must end today.

We are replacing reassurance with two powerful tools.

HACK 1 IS RADICAL VALIDATION

We call this the Magic Mirror technique.

Hack 2 is the Language Reset Protocol.

HACK 1: THE MAGIC MIRROR

When your child is panicking, their brain is screaming DANGER.

They are not rational.

They are stuck in their fight or flight system.

If you tell them, "Stop worrying," you are fighting their reality.

This makes them feel misunderstood.

It raises the volume on their fear, not lowers it.

Validation is simply reflecting their feeling back to them.

It is the Magic Mirror.

You are showing them that you see their pain clearly.

You are joining them emotionally, but not logically.

Validation sounds like this.

"Wow, you are feeling so incredibly scared right now."

"I see tears. This feels huge."

"Your heart is racing. That feeling is intense."

Notice what is missing.

There is no, "But you are safe."

There is no, "The dog won't bite you."

There is no, "It's just a test."

You are validating the emotion only.

You are validating the feeling state.

You are not validating the fear premise.

This is the critical difference.

When you validate the feeling, you lower the emotional tension.

They feel heard.

The anxiety monster thrives on isolation.

It whispers, "No one understands how scary this is."

Validation immediately breaks that isolation.

It shows them you are on their team.

This simple phrase, "I see that you are scared," can drop their core fear response by 60 percent.

It is like letting the steam out of a pressure cooker.

The pressure is still there, but the immediate crisis is lessened.

Now let's look at reassurance.

Reassurance is a compulsion you perform.

It is a mental checking ritual for you, the parent.

You say, "Are you sure we locked the door?"

You answer, "Yes, I checked it four times."

The child feels better for 30 seconds.

Then the anxiety troll demands another check.

The demand cycle never ends.

You must substitute reassurance entirely.

Instead of: "You are safe."

Say: "I see you feel unsafe right now."

Instead of: "It's only a little spider."

Say: "You are having a very strong fear reaction to that spider."

You are speaking the language of emotion.

You are not speaking the language of logic or safety guarantees.

Anxiety cannot be reasoned away.

It must be experienced and moved through.

Your validation is the firm handshake that guides them into the experience.

It is not the shield that keeps them from it.

Hack 1 is non-negotiable.

Practice it this afternoon.

The moment they show fear, validate the feeling.

Stop immediately before you give the safety guarantee.

Use the Magic Mirror.

Reflect the feeling.

Stop talking.

Wait for their reply.

HACK 2: THE LANGUAGE RESET PROTOCOL

This hack separates the child from the problem.

We learned in Chapter 2 that anxiety is a bully.

OCD is a demanding troll.

They are external entities.

They are not your child.

Your child is kind.

Your child is brave.

Your child is creative.

The fear is a noisy neighbour trying to take over the house.

We must train our language to reflect this separation always.

When a child says, "I can't do my homework," they internalize that failure.

They believe, "I am a person who cannot do homework."

This is devastating to their identity.

When you use the Language Reset, you flip the script.

You say, "The anxiety bully wants you to give up on that homework right now."

You shift the blame instantly.

The enemy is now external.

The child and the parent are united against the bully.

This is transformative.

It empowers them to fight back.

The fight is not against their own messy brain.

The fight is against a stupid bully that whispers lies.

This works powerfully for OCD rituals too.

If your child is checking the lock for the tenth time.

Do not say, "Stop checking the lock."

This feels like an attack on them.

Instead, use the language reset.

You must address the troll directly.

You say, "Oh, the OCD troll is demanding you check that again."

"What a bossy troll he is."

"Let's tell the troll, 'Not today.'"

You are giving the troll a name and a personality.

This process is called externalization.

It allows the child to step back from the intense feeling of being trapped by their own mind.

It creates necessary distance.

Think of your child as a brave knight.

The anxiety is a dragon outside the castle walls.

If the knight believes the dragon lives inside them, they feel hopeless.

If the knight sees the dragon outside, they can pick up their shield.

You are handing them the shield by changing your words.

Here are specific Language Reset scripts.

When the child refuses food due to fear of choking.

Do not say: "Just eat it, you won't choke." (Reassurance)

Say: "That fear bully is telling you a big lie about choking." (Separation)

Say: "We know that is the bully's voice." (Identification)

Say: "What small bite can you take to show the bully you are the boss?" (Action)

When the child is worried about germs or contamination.

Do not say: "The playground is clean." (Reassurance)

Say: "That germ troll wants you to believe the whole park is filthy." (Separation)

Say: "That troll is really good at making up stories." (Identification)

Say: "We are going to give the troll a short, bored look and go swing." (Action)

The tone is essential here.

It must be playful but firm.

You are conveying confidence in the face of their struggle.

You are not arguing with the reality of their feelings.

You are arguing with the reality of the bully's demands.

This combination of Hack 1 and Hack 2 is your immediate priority.

You use validation first.

The fear spikes.

You use the Magic Mirror.

"I see you are terrified of leaving the house."

The fear slightly drops because they feel heard.

Then you immediately pivot to Hack 2.

"That is the anxiety bully making up rules about our family."

"We don't let bullies make our family rules."

This two-step process achieves several things simultaneously.

First, it honors their emotional state.

Second, it prevents you from falling into the reassurance trap.

Third, it gives the child a tangible target for their internal fight.

They are fighting the externalized anxiety.

They are not fighting their own worth.

A key part of the Language Reset is consistency.

If you are the only one calling it the bully, the system breaks down.

You must explain this concept to your child clearly.

Do this when they are calm.

Sit down and define the enemy together.

What does the bully look like?

Is it green?

Does it wear a stupid hat?

What is its favorite lie?

Giving the anxiety a ridiculous, concrete form makes it less powerful.

It makes it childish.

The scariest monsters are the nameless ones in the dark.

We are putting a name tag and a spotlight on this monster.

When your child uses fearful language, you gently redirect them.

If they say, "I am scared of the dark."

You reply, "That's the darkness bully talking. What do you want to tell him?"

This trains the child to use the language themselves.

It creates the Resilience Shield we will talk about later.

They start saying, "Mom, the worry thoughts are telling me I need to wash my hands again."

This is a massive win.

They are identifying the threat.

They are separating from the contamination.

They are asking you for coaching against the bully, not for permission to avoid.

This is the shift from patient to warrior.

Your role shifts too.

You move from caretaker to coach.

Coaches acknowledge pain.

Coaches validate the effort.

Coaches never do the work for the athlete.

Coaches certainly never agree with the opponent.

Your coach response is validation followed by separation and action.

Validation.

"I know how heavy that fear feels right now."

Separation.

"That is the anxiety bully trying to convince you to stay home."

Action.

"What is the smallest thing we can do right now to make the bully mad?"

This is the core communication style for the rest of this program.

It may feel odd at first.

It may feel unnatural to stop saying, "It will be okay."

Your child may resist the language reset initially.

They might say, "It's not the troll, Mom. I really need to check the door."

This is resistance from the fear system.

It is the bully trying to protect itself.

Be unwavering.

Be gentle but firm.

Respond with more validation and separation.

"I understand it feels like it is really you who needs to check."

"That is how sneaky the OCD troll is. It tricks you into thinking it is your idea."

"But we know better now. We are the boss of the door, not the troll."

Hold this line.

The goal is to provide empathy without providing the reward of avoidance or reassurance.

Reassurance is a quick fix that perpetuates long-term suffering.

Validation is a harder, slower approach that builds long-term resilience.

It is the difference between giving a starving person a tiny piece of chocolate or teaching them how to farm.

We are farming resilience in your living room.

Start using the Magic Mirror validation today.

Start labelling the bully immediately.

This simple language shift will prepare your child for the bigger steps coming next.

The next steps involve action.

Action is exposure.

The Language Reset makes exposure possible.

It creates a common enemy that you both can face.

You are the unyielding, validating coach.

You are ready for the next move.

That next move is being the rock during the actual panic.

That is Hack 3.

Let's get ready to anchor the storm.

CHAPTER FOUR

—★-★-★—

HACK 3 & 4: THE 'UNFLAPPABLE ANCHOR' STRATEGY: HOW TO SHUT DOWN A FULL-BLOWN PANIC ATTACK IN 90 SECONDS... PLUS, THE BLUEPRINT FOR THE PARENT-LED FEAR LADDER (VALUE: $497)

You are exhausted by the drama.

Every parent who has seen their child crumble knows this feeling.

The fear response hits like a tsunami.

It is sudden.

It is loud.

It is terrifying for everyone involved.

Your child is screaming that they cannot breathe.

They are shaking uncontrollably.

They are convinced they are dying or going crazy.

Your heart pounds right along with theirs.

This is the moment most parents fail the test.

I say that with compassion, not judgment.

You fail the test because your natural, loving instinct takes over.

You rush in to fix it.

You start talking fast.

You ask a dozen questions.

Are you okay.

What happened.

Breathe for me.

Slow down.

Stop crying.

You try to logically dismantle the panic attack right in the middle of a chemical storm.

This is exactly the wrong thing to do.

It backfires every single time.

It is Hack 3 we deploy in these critical 90 seconds.

This is the Unflappable Anchor Strategy.

This hack shifts your role entirely.

You stop being the frantic medic trying to stop the bleeding.

You become the immovable rock in the center of the storm.

Your child's brain is looking for data points.

It is trying to confirm if the fear it is generating is true fear.

Is there a tiger in the room.

Is this danger real.

When you panic, you confirm the danger.

Your high, fast voice says, yes, something is terribly wrong.

Your rushing movement says, yes, we need to escape immediately.

Your anxiety mirrors their anxiety.

The system spirals upward instantly.

To shut down a panic attack, you must present an alternative data point.

You must become the proof that the environment is safe.

This requires acting.

It requires physical control on your part.

When the panic hits, you must pause for two seconds before reacting.

Ground your feet firmly into the floor.

Drop your shoulders.

Lower the volume and pitch of your voice.

This is non-negotiable.

Your child needs to hear a deep, slow resonance of certainty.

When you speak, use the absolute minimum number of words possible.

Do not ask questions.

Do not try to find the cause of the panic.

The cause is irrelevant right now.

The treatment is your calm.

Here is the 90-second script for the Unflappable Anchor.

Step one. Get physically low.

If your child is on the floor, you sit on the floor nearby.

Do not hover over them.

This minimizes the threat perception.

Step two. Use one line of validation.

I see you are having a panic attack.

I see you are scared.

That is all you say.

No 'It is okay' or 'You are safe' yet.

Just acknowledgment without drama.

Step three. State the biological truth neutrally.

Your brain thinks we are running from a bear.

Your body is working hard.

It will pass.

Step four. The Anchor statement.

I am right here.

I am calm.

I am staying right here until this is over.

You do not need to do anything.

Just feel the feelings.

Then you stop talking.

The crucial move in this hack is the silence that follows.

You wait.

You become the silent witness.

You do not guide their breathing.

The instruction to breathe deeper often makes them feel suffocated.

You do not touch them unless they specifically ask for comfort.

Physical contact during panic can sometimes increase the sense of being trapped.

You just sit there.

You breathe slowly yourself.

Your slow breathing is the only thing they should notice.

Their body language will start to match yours.

They watch you.

You are showing them that this feeling, this terror, is temporary.

It is manageable.

It is not an emergency for you.

Therefore, it is not a fatal emergency for them.

This unwavering calm is a form of exposure therapy itself.

They are exposed to the feeling of panic.

They are exposed to the urge to escape.

But they cannot escape because you, the anchor, are not moving.

They learn in that moment that they can survive the feeling.

They learn it from watching your complete lack of reaction.

Remember the goal is not stopping the panic immediately.

The goal is showing them that they are safe even while the panic is happening.

This reduces the secondary panic, the fear of the fear itself.

Hack 3 sets the stage for Hack 4.

Hack 4 is the Parent-Led Fear Ladder.

We have spent the last few chapters talking about avoiding avoidance.

We know that avoidance is the fuel source for anxiety.

Every time your child avoids something scary, the anxiety monster gets stronger.

If we are going to defeat the bully, we have to face it down.

We do this systematically.

We do not just throw them into the deep end.

We use the Fear Ladder.

This blueprint is often called an Exposure Hierarchy in therapy.

It is the single most potent tool in cognitive behavioral treatment for anxiety and OCD.

And the parent must be the chief architect.

If you leave this to the child, they will either make the steps too easy or too impossible.

We need goldilocks exposures.

Just right.

The Fear Ladder takes a massive, overwhelming fear and breaks it down into bite-sized, digestible steps.

Think of it like climbing a skyscraper.

You do not jump from the ground floor to the hundredth floor.

You take the elevator one floor at a time.

This structured process removes the unpredictability of exposure.

Anxiety hates predictability.

It thrives in the chaotic unknown.

We are taking away that power.

The first step in building the ladder is identifying the target.

What is the biggest thing the anxiety or OCD troll is demanding or avoiding.

Is it sleeping alone.

Is it touching certain surfaces.

Is it going to school.

Is it separation from you.

Let us use separation anxiety as our example.

The ultimate goal, the top of the ladder, is 100 on the fear scale.

That is, staying overnight at Grandma's house with you nowhere near.

That is the high dive.

We start at the wading pool.

You need to list out ten to fifteen steps leading up to that goal.

This is a brainstorming session for you, the parent.

Do not involve the child yet in the creation.

You are the coach writing the plays.

You use a Subjective Units of Distress Scale, or SUDS, to rate each step.

Zero is no anxiety.

One hundred is full-blown panic.

Your starting exposures should be rated 20 to 30.

They must be uncomfortable, but doable.

For separation anxiety, a step 20 might be Mom standing outside the bedroom door for five minutes while the child plays alone inside.

A step 30 might be Mom sitting in the car outside the house for ten minutes while the child stays inside with the sitter.

A step 50 is Mom running a quick errand for 30 minutes.

A step 70 is Mom gone for two hours to a movie.

You write down every single step.

You create a visual roadmap.

The child needs to see where they are going.

This transparency builds trust in your process.

Once the ladder is built, you present it to your child not as a punishment, but as a map to freedom.

You frame it using the Hack 2 language.

We are going to make the anxiety monster very bored.

We are going to teach the bully that we are the boss now.

We are going to climb this ladder together.

The second part of Hack 4 is the crucial execution rule.

The rule is choice within structure.

The child does not get to choose if we do an exposure today.

They get to choose which exposure we do today.

This gives them a sense of autonomy.

They are choosing the fight, not having it forced on them entirely.

You tell them, we must do one step on the ladder today.

Do you want to do step two or step three.

We are not going backwards.

We are only moving up.

Once you commit to a step, there are two golden rules.

Rule one. No reassurance during the exposure.

We already covered this in detail.

The child must sit in the fear without being rescued by your words.

Rule two. The exposure is non-negotiable once it starts.

You cannot let them quit halfway through.

If the step is sitting in the car alone for ten minutes, you sit out that ten minutes.

Even if they are crying at minute seven.

If you cave, you teach them that crying harder is the escape route.

You teach the anxiety monster that if it fights hard enough, it wins.

We cannot afford that loss.

This is where the Unflappable Anchor comes back into play.

You are leading the ladder.

You are the one setting the time limit.

When the anxiety spikes mid-exposure, you are calm.

You use the same slow, quiet voice.

I see you are scared right now.

We have three more minutes on this step.

We are staying strong.

Then you return to silence.

The exposure is only successful when the child stays in the situation long enough for the anxiety to naturally subside.

We call this habituation.

That is the secret to brain rewiring we will cover fully in the next chapter.

But for now, understand the practical outcome.

If the fear level starts at 30, we must stay there until it drops below 15.

That is the proof that the brain is adapting.

That is the proof that the fear circuit is breaking.

Your job as the coach is to make sure they complete the duration of the task, whatever the cost in temporary discomfort.

Remember, you are prioritizing long-term emotional freedom over short-term peace.

This is a professional battle plan.

It is systematic.

It is parent-led.

It is structured.

The Fear Ladder is the path out of avoidance.

The Unflappable Anchor is the mindset that makes the climb possible.

You provide the safety.

They provide the effort.

You are ready to map out your child's ascent toward resilience.

You are the solution.

CHAPTER FIVE

—★-★-★—

HACK 5 & 6: THE 7-MINUTE BRAIN REWIRING SECRET - HOW TO FORCE THE ANXIETY CIRCUIT TO SELF-DESTRUCT... AND THE 3 SCRIPTS FOR BLOCKING COMPULSIVE RITUALS WITHOUT STARTING A WAR

This is where the real power starts.

We have handled the language.

We have handled your calm.

We have created the roadmap for fear.

Now we must execute the science.

We are going to teach your child's brain to self-destruct the fear circuit.

This is Hack 5.

Hack 5 is called Habituation.

It is the most critical concept in treating anxiety.

It sounds complex.

It is unbelievably simple.

It is the 7-Minute Brain Rewiring Secret.

Think about a smell.

When you walk into a bakery, the scent of fresh bread is overwhelming.

It is strong.

Your senses are flooded.

After five minutes of being inside, what happens?

The smell fades.

You stop noticing it.

It is still there, but your brain has decided it is not a threat.

Your brain has decided it is not new information.

It habituated.

The same exact thing happens with fear.

Anxiety is a feeling of threat.

It is a massive spike of adrenaline.

It is a fire alarm going off in the brain.

It is loud.

It is terrifying.

It demands immediate attention.

When your child starts an exposure task, or when they face a fear they usually avoid, the alarm sounds.

It sounds instantly.

Their anxiety score shoots up to a 9 or a 10.

It feels unbearable.

This is the moment of truth.

The natural, panicked reaction is to run away.

The child wants to escape the bakery.

They want to leave the room.

They want to wash their hands immediately.

They want to check the lock one more time.

They want the relief.

This relief is called avoidance.

Avoidance instantly drops the anxiety score back down to a 2.

The brain learns a dangerous lesson right then.

It learns, "My alarm system saved me."

It learns, "The fear was real, and escape was necessary."

The fear circuit gets stronger.

Now look at habituation.

You keep your child in the fear situation.

You use Hack 3, The Unflappable Anchor, to remain completely calm.

You hold the line.

Your child is distressed.

They are shouting.

They are melting down.

But you do not let them avoid.

You keep them in the bakery.

The adrenaline spike is designed to be temporary.

It is an exhausting state for the body.

It cannot be sustained for long.

The body simply runs out of fuel for that intense panic.

If your child stays in that 9/10 fear zone, without running away or seeking a ritual, their brain realizes something profound.

It realizes, "The danger signal is wrong."

It realizes, "I am still here. I am safe. I did not die."

This is the 7-minute secret.

For most children, the initial terror spike hits its peak and begins to drop within 7 to 10 minutes.

It might take longer sometimes.

But the drop is guaranteed.

The only way to stop the drop is to leave the situation or perform a ritual.

We are teaching the brain to see the false alarm through to the end.

The anxiety decreases naturally.

The child experiences relief not because they ran away, but because they endured.

They stood their ground.

This is how the anxiety circuit self-destructs.

It starves itself of the payoff.

The payoff is relief from avoidance.

Your job as the parent is the clock watcher.

You are the time keeper.

When they are screaming about the spider drawing, or the dirty doorknob, or the thought of a disaster.

You look at the clock.

You say, "I see the Monster is making you very upset. We are staying right here until the Monster gets bored."

Then you wait 7 minutes.

You do not engage with the fear content.

You only engage with the courage.

When they feel the first drop in anxiety, even from a 9 to an 8, that is the chemical proof of safety.

You reinforce that moment.

"Did you feel that small shift? That was your courage winning."

This is the fundamental mechanism of exposure therapy.

We are using the brain's natural capacity to adapt.

If it is exposed to something frightening and nothing bad happens, the brain eventually tags that thing as safe.

It is the most powerful tool you own.

But it requires firmness.

It requires holding your child in discomfort long enough for the magic 7 minutes to pass.

This brings us directly to Hack 6.

We must aggressively block the avoidance mechanism.

When anxiety is present, avoidance looks like running away from a dog.

When OCD is present, avoidance looks like performing a compulsive ritual.

Hack 6 is Ritual Blocking.

If Hack 5 is the theory of endurance, Hack 6 is the practical warfare against the Troll.

Remember the difference.

Anxiety is the feeling.

The Bully demands you avoid things like parties or crowds.

OCD is the cycle.

The Troll forces an obsession, a terrifying thought.

Then it demands a ritual, a compulsive action, to temporarily neutralize the terror.

Washing hands 10 times is the ritual.

Checking the stove 4 times is the ritual.

Asking, "Are you sure I won't get sick?" three times is the ritual.

These rituals are the oxygen supply for the OCD Troll.

If you let your child perform the ritual, you just enabled the Troll.

The fear drops temporarily.

The circuit strengthens permanently.

You must block the ritual every single time.

One hundred percent of the time.

No exceptions.

A single exception teaches the brain that if they fight hard enough, the ritual will happen.

This is the hardest part for most parents.

It feels mean.

It feels counterintuitive.

You are blocking their only perceived source of relief.

You must remember you are blocking a behavior.

You are not blocking their feelings.

You validate the distress.

You block the compulsion.

How do you block a compulsive ritual without starting a war?

It requires preparation and three specific scripts.

Script 1: The Acknowledgment and Deflection (For Reassurance Seeking).

Reassurance seeking is the most common and damaging ritual.

It is obsessive question asking.

"Is the door locked?"

"Are you sure the cat is okay?"

"Did I finish my homework right?"

"Is it guaranteed we won't crash the car?"

Your natural parent instinct is to answer the question.

You want to soothe them.

You must resist this urge completely.

Answering the question is performing the ritual for them.

You are their co-conspirator.

Instead, use this script.

Child: "Mom, did I lock the front door? I have to check again."

Parent: "I hear the Troll making you feel like you need to check that door."

Parent: "I know that feeling is powerful right now."

Parent: "We already established that checking is the Troll's job."

Parent: "I am not going to help the Troll today."

Parent: "Your job is to feel that anxious feeling and remember we are doing Hack 5."

Parent: "Let's go read a book together instead."

You validate the feeling.

You label the source (the Troll or the Monster).

You explicitly refuse the ritual.

You offer a redirection into a non-anxiety activity.

You must be a broken record.

They will ask again.

You will give the exact same response.

Be patient, but unwavering.

Script 2: The Gentle but Firm Refusal (For Physical Rituals).

This applies to hand washing, touching things multiple times, excessive arranging, or repeating phrases.

These are often more visible.

They are easier to block, but the resulting meltdown is often more intense.

Example: A child insists on washing hands for three minutes after touching a remote control.

Parent: "I see you are worried about the remote control."

Parent: "We are washing our hands for 30 seconds today."

Child: "No! I need longer! It's still dirty!"

Parent: "I know the Troll is telling you that."

Parent: "We are finished with hand washing for now."

Parent: (Physically but gently redirecting them away from the sink).

Parent: "I am in charge of the hand washing rules."

Parent: "You are in charge of practicing your courage."

You are setting the rule firmly.

You are acknowledging their inner distress ("I know the Troll is telling you that").

You are providing the immediate limit.

You are physically blocking the compulsion if necessary, without being aggressive.

Your tone must remain absolutely calm.

This models Hack 3.

If the ritual involves extreme arranging or organizing, you might have to say, "I am sorry, but the Troll does not get to dictate how our toys are lined up."

You must intentionally tolerate the mess or the perceived wrongness.

The child needs to experience the anxiety spike caused by the uncompleted ritual.

Then they need to see that nothing bad happens.

This is Hack 5 in action.

Script 3: The Time-Based Delay (The Compromise Strategy).

Sometimes, a full, immediate block leads to violence or extreme distress that is overwhelming for the parent to manage initially.

This script is a strategic delay.

It is especially helpful for checking rituals or minor organizational compulsions.

Delay is not denial, but it breaks the immediate, addictive feedback loop of the ritual.

Child: "I need to go back inside and check the stove right now."

Parent: "The stove check is coming."

Parent: "The Troll needs to wait 10 minutes first."

Parent: "We are driving around the block two times, and then we will talk about the stove."

The goal is to introduce a gap between the anxiety spike and the relief behavior.

If the child agrees to the delay, the anxiety naturally begins to drop during those 10 minutes (Hack 5).

When 10 minutes are up, the parent then says, "Okay, the time is up. How high is the worry now?"

Often, the anxiety has dropped from a 9 to a 6 or 7.

Then the parent says, "Great. You just proved you do not need to check. You beat the Troll for 10 minutes. Let's double that time."

If they cannot wait 10 minutes, you might start with 3 minutes.

The key is incremental increase.

You are demanding they tolerate the initial panic spike without the usual quick fix.

This entire process of Ritual Blocking is the opposite of enabling.

It is challenging the Troll directly.

It is compassionate.

It is confident.

It is the only way to prove to your child's brain that the ritual is not a necessity for safety.

It is only a temporary drug for anxiety.

We are detoxing the brain from that drug.

These two hacks, Habituation and Ritual Blocking, are the core of the treatment.

Hack 5 is the mechanism of change.

Hack 6 is the application of change.

You must put your foot down.

You must be the authority on safety.

You are the boss of the rituals now.

You will see major resistance at first.

This is proof the hacks are working.

You are starving the Monster.

It is throwing a tantrum because it is losing its food supply.

Hold the line.

Remember the 7-minute secret.

Relief is coming, but only after they endure the peak.

CHAPTER SIX

—★-★-★—

HACK 7 & 8: THE REASSURANCE TRAP - WHY 'ARE YOU SURE WE'RE SAFE?' IS A POISON PILL... PLUS, THE 4 NON-NEGOTIABLE RULES THAT STOP ANXIETY FROM DICTATING YOUR FAMILY SCHEDULE

This is the most dangerous hack.

It is dangerous because it feels wrong.

It asks you to do the opposite of what every single parenting instinct tells you to do.

It asks you to withhold comfort.

It asks you to deny peace.

But that peace is fake.

That comfort is a lie.

We are talking about Hack 7.

This is the Reassurance TRAP.

Reassurance is the poison pill of anxiety parenting.

It is subtle.

It looks like love.

It sounds like responsibility.

Your child asks you a question.

Are you sure the stove is off.

Did you lock the car door.

Is that headache cancer.

Is that stain on my shirt permanent.

Is the neighbor's dog safe.

Your automatic, loving, protective response is always Yes.

Of course, honey.

I checked it twice.

Everything is fine.

Your child feels immediate relief.

They exhale.

You exhale.

The moment is over.

But the anxiety bully just won a major battle.

Reassurance is not a solution.

It is a compulsion disguised as a question.

It functions exactly the same way as checking the stove ten times or washing hands until they crack.

It is a ritual.

The child feels a jolt of uncertainty or fear.

They perform a ritual.

The ritual provides a temporary sense of control or safety.

That temporary feeling reinforces the belief that the fear was real.

It proves that the ritual saved them.

Asking you for safety confirmation is their ritual.

You providing the answer is their temporary safety net.

You are training their brain to believe that they cannot tolerate uncertainty.

You are training their brain to believe that you are the only source of safety.

This is a disastrous cycle for independence.

It is a relentless cycle for parents.

You cannot possibly guarantee safety twenty-four hours a day.

You cannot become a human safety monitor.

We have to cut the oxygen supply to the Reassurance Bully.

We have to stop answering the question.

This does not mean you are cold.

It means you are confident.

It means you are transferring the responsibility for tolerating uncertainty back to the child.

They need to learn that the feeling of needing certainty is temporary.

They need to learn that they can handle the distress that comes from not knowing.

This is the cornerstone of cognitive behavioral therapy.

The parent must stop accommodating the fear.

So, how do we stop the reassurance trap?

We employ deflection scripts.

These scripts must be memorized.

They must be delivered with the calm, unflappable energy of Hack 3.

You are not annoyed.

You are simply stating a fact.

You are a broken record of non-reassurance.

First, identify the question as an anxiety demand.

A question is an anxiety demand if it has been asked before.

A question is an anxiety demand if it asks you to guarantee a future outcome.

A question is an anxiety demand if it asks you to check or verify something that is low risk.

When the demand comes, you pivot immediately.

You do not engage the content.

You engage the underlying fear.

Let's look at some examples of the scripts you must use.

The child asks, Mom, are you sure that car light was green.

You respond, That sounds like the Anxiety Bully looking for a snack.

The child asks, I think I heard a noise. Is everyone safe in this house.

You respond, I see the fear monster is trying to get me to do its job.

The child asks, I feel sick. Is this going to be serious.

You respond, That is a tough feeling. You can handle that feeling without checking.

The key is repetition and simplicity.

You use the scripts to redirect their attention away from the content of the fear and toward the mechanism of the fear.

You are not dismissing their feeling.

You are validating their effort to perform a ritual.

Hack 1 told us to validate the emotion.

I see you are scared.

I know you are worried.

Then we apply Hack 7.

I know you are worried, but I am not going to give the worry monster the answer it wants.

That is how you merge the hacks.

It is loving validation followed by firm boundary setting.

The child will push back.

They will escalate.

They are used to the quick hit of relief.

They will try harder to get you to crack.

This is normal.

This is the extinction burst.

You must hold the line.

You must be the Anchor.

If you give in after forty minutes of crying, you have taught them a terrible lesson.

You have taught them that forty minutes of escalation gets them the answer.

You must cut it off quickly.

The broken record approach works best.

I already told you that I am not discussing that with the Bully.

I love you.

I am done talking about it.

Go draw a picture of the Bully instead.

Or, Here is a good one for older kids.

When they ask, Did I lock the door.

You respond, What does the Anxiety Troll say I should do.

They say, Tell me that you locked it.

You say, Right. And what are we supposed to tell the Troll.

They say, To stop asking.

You say, Exactly.

You are forcing them to practice their coping skills using your deflection as the trigger.

You are transferring the internal dialogue from Parent-to-Child to Child-to-Anxiety.

This is powerful liberation for you and for them.

Now we move to Hack 8.

Hack 8 is Confident Boundary Setting.

If Hack 7 is about microscopic interactions, Hack 8 is about the macro structure of family life.

Anxiety is an expert negotiator.

It demands accommodations.

It seeks to shrink the world of the family until it is tiny and controllable.

If you let the anxiety monster dictate your schedule, you are not living.

You are surviving its commands.

The goal of this hack is to install four non-negotiable rules.

These rules function like fixed stars in the night sky.

They are stable.

They do not move.

They provide safety not because they guarantee outcomes, but because they guarantee predictability.

Rule 1 is No One Else Performs the Ritual.

This is about preventing family members from enabling the cycle.

If your child has contamination OCD, other family members may start cleaning things for them.

If your child has separation anxiety, the other parent may avoid date night.

If your child is a checker, siblings may start checking things and reporting back.

This is accommodation.

It is dangerous.

The rule is simple.

We are helping you fight the monster.

We will not help the monster fight you.

Every family member must agree to this rule.

If your spouse picks up the ritual, they are undoing your hard work.

If Grandma checks the electrical outlets when she visits, she is feeding the Bully.

Your role as the parent-as-treatment-leader is to enforce this rule across the board.

Rule 2 is Anxiety Does Not Cancel Plans.

This is about preventing avoidance.

Avoidance is the core mechanism of anxiety maintenance.

If your child is anxious about a school play, an outing, or a sleepover, the temptation is to let them skip it.

It feels kind.

It feels gentle.

It is deadly to recovery.

When you allow avoidance, you confirm the danger.

You teach the brain that the situation was indeed too risky.

The rule states that unless the child has a raging fever or a broken bone, the plan proceeds as scheduled.

We can proceed scared.

We can proceed crying.

But we proceed.

Your job is to be the confident co-pilot.

I know this is hard.

We are going anyway.

You are strong enough to feel scared and still participate.

This must be non-negotiable.

Rule 3 is Sleep Happens in Your Bed.

This boundary is crucial for many families struggling with separation anxiety or fear of the dark.

The child often demands to sleep with parents.

This is a powerful accommodation that destroys sleep quality and parental intimacy.

If anxiety is dictating your sleeping arrangements, it has taken over too much territory.

The rule is set in stone.

Once the child is old enough to be sleeping independently, that is where they sleep.

If they come into your room in the middle of the night, you have a specific, scripted response.

I love you.

I know you are scared.

You can handle being scared.

It is time to go back to your own bed.

You gently walk them back.

You do not argue.

You do not lecture.

You do not get pulled into the reassurance trap.

If they keep returning, you calmly walk them back every single time until they stay.

This might mean three sleepless nights for you.

But those three nights purchase years of peace and independence later.

It is an investment.

Rule 4 is No Repetitive Questioning After One Clear Answer.

This ties back directly to Hack 7 but solidifies it as a structural family rule.

The anxious child may ask the same question five times in five minutes.

We already established that you stop answering the content.

The boundary rule states that after the deflection script is used once, the conversation is closed.

If the child continues to press, a boundary consequence must follow.

This is not punishment.

It is the necessary removal of attention or privilege that enables the cycle.

Example.

Child asks for reassurance for the fifth time while you are reading a book together.

You use the deflection script.

I am not talking to the Bully.

The child immediately asks again.

You look them in the eye, calmly.

I have answered you.

I am not going to talk about this again.

If you ask again, our reading time ends for the night.

If they ask a seventh time, you close the book immediately.

You maintain calm.

You remove the desired attention.

You say, I see you chose to ask again.

Reading time is over.

We can try again tomorrow when the Bully stays quiet.

This is incredibly hard.

It will bring tears.

It will bring anger.

But you are the leader of the family.

You are setting the structure.

You are the confident coach.

You are teaching them that anxiety does not get to run the house.

It gets to exist.

It does not get to control.

By setting these four non-negotiable boundaries, you reclaim massive amounts of family territory.

You reclaim your peace.

You reclaim your right to a life not dictated by fear.

This action is therapy.

This is how you win.

CHAPTER SEVEN

HACK 9: THE 'NO SABOTAGE' PROTOCOL - HOW TO MAKE SIBLINGS, GRANDPARENTS, AND TEACHERS ENFORCE YOUR PLAN (STOP INCONSISTENT RESPONSES FROM DERAILING 6 WEEKS OF PROGRESS)

You are making massive strides.

You are blocking the rituals at home.

You are using the validation scripts.

You are being the unflappable anchor.

The fear monster is shrinking.

It is noticing that your walls are solid.

But the monster is sneaky.

It knows you leave the house sometimes.

It knows there are other helpers.

It starts looking for loopholes.

It seeks out the cracks in your fortress.

This is the sabotage factor.

It is the single biggest threat to your child's recovery.

It is why Hack 9 is non-negotiable.

The No Sabotage Protocol is about consistency.

It is about getting every adult on the same page.

If you work for six weeks to stop reassurance, that work is immediately wiped out.

It happens the moment Grandma gives in.

It happens the second the teacher allows the child to skip the presentation.

Inconsistency teaches your child a dangerous lesson.

It teaches them that persistence pays off.

If they push the anxiety hard enough, they will find an accommodating adult.

They will find the easy path.

We must close the easy path entirely.

The treatment only works when the entire system is united.

You must become the Chief Executive Officer of this treatment plan.

Everyone else is supporting staff.

They must follow your directives.

The most difficult conversations often happen right at home.

We need to start with your primary co-parent or spouse.

You might think you are aligned.

But look closely at the nightly routine.

Is one of you secretly checking the stove one last time?

Is one of you rushing to soothe louder than the other?

Does one parent always take the anxious bedtime routine?

If there is a difference, the child knows.

They will exploit it ruthlessly.

You must schedule a specific, focused meeting with your partner.

This is not a casual chat over dinner.

This is a board meeting about treatment integrity.

Bring the science.

Explain what you have learned about enabling.

Explain that avoiding fear is not love.

It is enabling the fear.

Say clearly, "We are now both professional exposure coaches."

"We must speak exactly the same language."

"If I say no to a checking ritual, you must also say no."

"If I am being the anchor, you must not rush in with a life raft."

If your partner is struggling, help them practice the scripts.

Make them the Unflappable Anchor for five minutes a day.

Practice saying, "That is the Monster talking. I know you can ignore it."

Ensure they understand that the temporary peace gained from accommodating the anxiety leads to lifelong dependence.

Their love must be firm.

Their response must be predictable.

That predictability is therapeutic.

Any disagreement between parents, even subtle nonverbal signals, becomes a potential entry point for the Anxiety Bully.

Stop the loophole today.

Now we move to the next key group.

The siblings.

Anxiety often creates resentment in siblings.

They see the anxious child getting special treatment.

They see the attention lavished during meltdowns.

They are told to be quiet or to accommodate the fear.

This is damaging to the relationship.

It also enrolls the siblings into the cycle of enabling.

They might help with OCD rituals just to get it over with.

They might avoid certain games to prevent a meltdown.

We need to enlist them as allies, not passive victims.

Talk to your other children honestly but simply.

Do not overwhelm them with clinical terms.

Use the Monster metaphor.

Say, "Your brother is fighting a tough internal battle."

"We are teaching him how to be stronger than the Monster."

"When he asks you to re-check the lights, he is feeding the Monster."

"We need your help to starve it."

Give them very specific instructions.

Their role is not to be a therapist.

Their role is to be boring and unhelpful regarding the anxiety.

Here is the script for siblings.

"When Liam asks you if the oven is off, you say, 'That sounds like a question for the Monster. I am talking about soccer.'"

"When Emma asks you to hold her hand because the floor is 'sticky,' you say, 'I am busy. Your hands are perfectly clean.'"

Teach them to pivot the conversation immediately.

Anxiety craves attention.

Teach the siblings to give zero attention to the fear, but tons of attention to the child doing brave things.

"Wow, you went into the basement without asking me three times. That is huge."

Reward the siblings for their consistency.

Acknowledge that it is hard for them too.

Make it a family mission to defeat the Monster.

Next up are the landmines.

The loving saboteurs.

Grandparents and other occasional caretakers.

This is where progress often dies a swift death.

Grandparents operate from a place of deep, protective love.

They see distress and they want to eradicate it instantly.

They believe they are helping by stepping in.

They will rush to reassure.

They will stay the night because the child is scared.

They will allow avoidance because 'it is just easier for everyone.'

You must approach this conversation with maximum respect but unflinching firmness.

This is not a suggestion.

This is a medically necessary protocol.

Do not ask them if they agree with your parenting style.

State the requirement of the treatment plan.

You are informing them of the rules of the house and the recovery program.

You need to clearly communicate what you need them to stop doing.

Stop giving reassurance.

Stop participating in rituals.

Stop changing plans due to fear.

Provide them with the specific phrasing they must use.

Keep the script simple for them.

They need one or two lines they can fall back on automatically.

Script for Grandparents and Caretakers:

"Mom, we have started an intense treatment program for Sarah's anxiety."

"The experts are very clear that accommodation is preventing her from getting better."

"We need your absolute support on this."

"If she asks you, 'Are we going to be okay?' we need you to say, 'I know you feel unsure right now. I have total confidence in you.'"

"Do not engage with the content of the fear."

"Do not tell her she is safe."

"Just validate the feeling and move on."

Be prepared for pushback.

They might say you are being too hard.

They might say you are damaging her trust.

Your response must be calm and unwavering.

"I understand this feels counterintuitive, but this is the necessary path for her long-term freedom."

"We cannot accept any deviation from the plan."

"If consistency cannot be guaranteed, we will need to change the visitation structure temporarily."

That last line is harsh.

But it is vital.

You must protect the sanctity of the treatment.

The final perimeter defense is the school system.

Teachers and school counselors are essential partners.

But they are trained to nurture and accommodate students.

Often, anxiety accommodations are standard practice.

Allowing late submissions.

Permitting excessive trips to the nurse.

Letting the child call home five times a day.

These accommodations are accidental sabotage.

They teach the child that fear is a legitimate reason to escape difficulty.

School is where your child faces real-world exposures every day.

We must leverage that environment.

You need to schedule a meeting with the teacher and the counselor.

Send them a written summary of your protocol.

Use the phrase 'Parent-Led Exposure Response Prevention.'

This signals that you are running a therapeutic program, not just complaining about behavior.

Keep your instructions simple and practical for the school environment.

Focus on the three non-negotiables.

Non-Negotiable One: No phone calls home unless there is physical injury.

If the child is panicking, they must stay in the environment.

The panic attack must peak and subside without escape.

Script for Teacher: "I know you want to call her parents right now. But she is learning that this feeling passes. I need you to stay with her and say, 'I see you are very upset. You need to stay here until the end of class.'"

Non-Negotiable Two: No academic accommodations based on anxiety.

Fear is not an excuse to skip the presentation or the test.

The goal is brave behavior, not comfort.

Script for Teacher: "If she says she cannot take the test because she is nervous, please respond with, 'I know the worry monster is loud, but you need to sit and try your best for ten minutes. You have to finish this task.'"

Non-Negotiable Three: Zero reassurance regarding separation or safety.

The teacher must not offer comfort about Mom picking them up.

They should not verify safety protocols repeatedly.

Script for Teacher: "When she asks if she is going to get sick, respond with, 'That thought is not useful right now. Let's focus on geography.'"

Present this plan with confidence.

You are not dictating their job.

You are giving them the tools to help your child achieve independence.

Frame it as setting high expectations for resilience.

Most teachers will be relieved to have a clear, scientific mandate.

They are tired of the anxiety loop too.

Remember why this matters so much.

Every step your child takes toward bravery is a deposit in the confidence bank.

Every time an adult accommodates the fear, it is a withdrawal.

If you have five adults making consistent deposits, the balance grows quickly.

If you have one adult making huge withdrawals, you never get ahead.

The Monster thrives on chaos and mixed signals.

The No Sabotage Protocol demands crystal clear communication.

It demands courage from you to lead these adults.

It requires you to set the boundaries for your entire support network.

Be the uncompromising gatekeeper of your child's recovery.

Speak with one voice.

Act with one plan.

The consistency you build across the board is the protective shield that makes your child's recovery permanent.

Build that shield now.

CHAPTER EIGHT

HACK 10: THE 14-DAY RESILIENCE SHIELD - PREDICTING AND CRUSHING ANXIETY 'BLIPS' BEFORE THEY BECOME FULL-BLOWN RELAPSE (YOUR LONG-TERM FREEDOM STRATEGY)

YOU HAVE WORKED TIRELESSLY.

You have installed the initial nine hacks.

You are seeing success.

Maybe your child is sleeping through the night again.

Maybe they are attending school consistently.

Maybe the rituals are almost gone.

This is not luck.

This is the result of focused, confident parenting.

You broke the enabling cycle.

You earned this relief.

Now we face the critical phase.

Long-term freedom.

Recovery is rarely a straight line upward.

It looks like a messy, upward spiral.

There will be days that feel like a giant step back.

We call these setbacks 'blips'.

Hack 10 is your strategy for predicting and crushing these blips.

It is the 14-Day Resilience Shield.

This shield turns potential relapse into reinforced strength.

What is a blip.

A blip is a temporary spike in old anxiety patterns.

The anxiety monster does not surrender easily.

It retreats to the corner.

It recharges.

Then it tests the fence you built.

It throws out a fishing line of worry.

If you take the bait, the monster comes back roaring.

If you ignore the bait, the monster realizes its time is up.

Blips are usually tied to external stress.

They are short.

They are focused.

They are usually milder than the original crisis.

What is a relapse.

A relapse happens when the parent stops using the hacks.

A relapse happens when the parent panics during a blip.

A relapse happens when accommodations slowly creep back into the family routine.

The key difference is the parent's reaction.

The blip is the child's temporary discomfort.

The relapse is the family's return to dysfunction.

We are focused on preventing the relapse.

We do that by crushing every blip with speed and confidence.

The 14-Day Predictive Map

The first step of the Resilience Shield is looking ahead.

Anxiety loves surprises.

We must eliminate uncertainty where we can.

You need to become a trauma detective for your family calendar.

Look 14 days into the future right now.

What major events are looming.

Is there a big test at school.

Is there a doctor's appointment scheduled.

Are we taking a family trip.

Is a relative visiting.

Is your child getting a new teacher.

These transitions and uncertainties are red flags.

They signal potential weakness in the shield.

We anticipate these stress points.

We increase our mental readiness before the stress hits.

We also look for internal stress points.

These are less obvious.

They require detailed observation.

Is your child sick or fighting off a cold.

Tiredness is anxiety fuel.

A child who has missed two nights of sleep is a vulnerable child.

Is your child going through a growth spurt.

Are they navigating new social dynamics with friends.

A tired body and a stressed mind are easy targets for the anxiety bully.

We do not wait for the blip to appear.

We deploy the shield pre-emptively.

This means we reinforce the fundamental hacks starting today.

Pre-emptive Deployment Strategy.

When you see a stressor coming, you reinforce two things.

One. Hack 3. The Unflappable Anchor.

Two. Hack 6. Ritual Blocking.

If you know your child has a huge project presentation due Friday, anxiety will be high starting Tuesday.

Your voice needs to drop a register.

Your pace needs to slow down.

You need to be the physical embodiment of calm confidence starting Tuesday.

This models safety for their nervous system.

You are setting the tone before the fear spikes.

You are showing the anxiety that the leadership remains secure.

You are blocking the monster's path.

Next, you watch for the testing rituals.

Anxiety often returns via low-level requests for reassurance.

Did I do this assignment correctly.

Is this grade going to ruin everything.

Will the car be safe on the highway tomorrow.

These are tiny testing lines.

If you answer them fully, you feed the blip.

If you deflect them using the scripted responses from Hack 7, you crush the blip instantly.

I know you are worried about the project.

I have total confidence that you know how to handle the presentation.

We already talked about this.

That is the confidence switch.

The deflection is firm.

The deflection is predictable.

The Daily Data Shield.

We must stay objective during this long-term phase.

Anxiety is messy and emotional.

We use data to keep our feelings out of the equation.

During high-stress weeks, implement a simple tracking system.

Track three objective markers every single night.

One. Number of reassurance requests answered or deflected.

Two. Number of minutes spent in the Fear Ladder exposures.

Three. Number of family accommodations made.

If the reassurance number jumps from zero to ten in one day, that is a blip alert.

It is not a disaster.

It is data.

It tells you exactly where to deploy the force the next morning.

It stops the feeling of being overwhelmed.

You are managing metrics, not emotions.

The Rapid Response Protocol

When the blip occurs, the speed of your reaction is everything.

Do not think, 'Oh no, are we back to square one.'

Think, 'The anxiety monster is testing us, let's show it the door.'

You need to respond within seconds of the blip surfacing.

If your child starts a checking ritual, do not wait five minutes hoping it stops.

Immediately intervene with the scripts.

I see the anxiety troll is asking you to check the lock again.

We agreed we are not listening to that troll anymore.

The lock is fine.

Let's go read that book now.

This immediate response is key.

It prevents the anxiety circuit from fully activating.

It forces the circuit to self-destruct before it establishes a foothold.

The child receives immediate, consistent feedback.

Fear does not equal avoidance.

Using Blips as Exposure Practice.

Every blip is a gift.

It is a ready-made exposure.

If the blip focuses on returning fear of separation, use that moment.

The anxiety is already primed.

The fear is already present.

Do not retreat.

Do not coddle the anxiety.

Instead, use Hack 4.

Move immediately to a higher, focused step on the fear ladder related to that fear.

If they are anxious about leaving the house alone for ten minutes, tell them, 'The anxiety monster wants you to stay inside. We are going to defeat that plan. Go try for fifteen minutes instead.'

You are teaching them that setbacks are simply invitations for bigger bravery.

You are reframing the moment.

You are using the anxiety's own energy against it.

This is the power of resilience.

Teaching the Child Resilience Language.

Your child needs to understand what is happening internally.

They need the language to articulate their struggle without demanding reassurance.

When they express disappointment about feeling scared again, affirm the process, not the outcome.

It is okay to feel wobbly.

Wobbly means you are fighting.

It is totally normal to feel fear when there is stress at school.

Our job is not to eliminate fear.

Our job is to choose bravery over avoidance.

You chose bravery today when you walked into class.

That is the only metric that matters.

This shifts the goalpost.

The goal is not to feel calm.

The goal is to act despite the lack of calm.

This is the definition of true strength.

Maintaining the Boundary Fence.

The Resilience Shield relies on consistent boundaries.

Do not let old accommodations sneak back in because life got busy.

Maybe you used to check their homework every night.

You stopped that accommodation.

Now they have a huge project.

You might be tempted to jump back in and help 'just this once'.

Do not do it.

That 'just this once' is how the anxiety monster reclaims territory.

Hold the boundary.

Remind yourself that holding the line is the most loving thing you can do.

Your confidence is the only thing that sustains the gain.

Your consistency is their greatest treatment.

The Long-Term Mindset Shift.

Your goal is not a child who never worries.

That child does not exist.

Your goal is a child who worries, recognizes the feeling, deploys their self-management tools, and moves forward anyway.

You are teaching them self-efficacy.

You are teaching them agency.

You are handing them the keys to their own freedom.

You installed the hacks.

You modelled the calm.

You enforced the boundaries.

Now you must trust the process.

The blips will get smaller.

They will happen less often.

Eventually, your child will identify the blip themselves.

Mom, I think the bully is trying to get me to worry about the dentist appointment again.

That is the ultimate victory.

That is proof the shield is fully internalized.

You empowered them to recognize the enemy and deploy their own defense.

You are their confident coach now.

Keep looking 14 days ahead.

Keep deploying the hacks quickly and firmly.

Maintain the data.

You have the power to protect this freedom long-term.

This is your final hack.

This is your unwavering confidence in action.

Keep leading them to freedom.

CHAPTER NINE

—★-★-★—

THE ENABLING TRAPS: THE 5 'LOVING' ACTIONS THAT ARE SECRETLY FEEDING YOUR CHILD'S FEAR MONSTER EVERY SINGLE DAY

YOU LOVE YOUR CHILD FIERCELY.

This is not up for debate.

Your actions come from a place of deep, protective love.

You would literally step in front of a bus for them.

You have spent endless hours searching for answers.

You have spent money on therapists and programs.

You have done everything you can think of to ease their pain.

But sometimes the very things we do out of love become the tools of the anxiety monster.

They become the fuel that keeps the fear fire roaring.

We call these enabling traps.

They are subtle.

They feel gentle and necessary in the moment.

They look like parenting and they feel like compassion.

But functionally, they are proof to the child's brain that the world is indeed dangerous.

If the world were safe, you wouldn't have to change the rules for them, right.

The goal of this chapter is not to make you feel guilty.

It is to give you clarity.

It is to illuminate the shadows where anxiety hides its most powerful weapons.

We are going to identify the five most common traps.

Then we are going to learn how to gracefully, confidently, and lovingly withdraw from them.

TRAP 1: THE AVOIDANCE SHIELD

THIS IS THE MOST DANGEROUS TRAP OF ALL.

The Anxiety Monster thrives on avoidance.

If your child avoids something scary, the monster wins.

It gets stronger.

Avoidance is the temporary relief that guarantees long-term distress.

Parents often become the Chief Avoidance Officer.

You are constantly making small adjustments to shield your child from discomfort.

Maybe they refuse to attend playdates.

So you stop scheduling them.

Maybe they hate riding the bus because they worry about germs.

So you drive them to school every single day.

Maybe they are terrified of sleeping alone.

So you have slept on the floor of their room for three years now.

All of these actions are deeply loving.

They solve the immediate problem.

But they scream one message to your child's brain.

The threat is real.

I, the parent, confirm the threat is real because I am helping you escape it.

To withdraw from the Avoidance Shield, you must reverse accommodations slowly.

This is where the Fear Ladder (Hack 4) is critical.

You cannot go from sleeping on the floor to demanding they sleep alone tonight.

That is too aggressive.

It sets everyone up for failure.

Instead, define the accommodation.

Define the exposure goal.

Start small.

If you are sleeping on the floor, the first step is moving your sleeping bag to the door.

The next week, it moves to the hallway.

You validate their fear.

You say, "I see the monster wants me to stay here, but we are just showing the monster we are the leaders."

You stay calm.

You do not retreat.

You break the Avoidance Shield into tiny, manageable pieces.

TRAP 2: THE INSTANT PROBLEM SOLVER

An anxious child, especially one with OCD, can get stuck in a loop.

They worry about the smallest mistake.

They demand perfection.

They forget a homework assignment.

They forget their jacket.

They struggle with a simple puzzle.

Your instinct is to race in and fix it immediately.

You rush the forgotten item to school.

You complete the complex Lego build for them.

You call the teacher and negotiate a deadline extension because they had a meltdown the night before.

When you rush in, you steal two vital tools from your child.

You steal their ability to tolerate distress.

You steal their ability to solve problems.

They learn that if they worry loudly enough, a rescuer will appear.

This teaches helplessness.

It tells them that they are too fragile to handle normal disappointment or minor mistakes.

To withdraw from the Instant Problem Solver trap, you must introduce the delay tactic.

If they call you at work needing something, respond with a boundary.

Say, "That sounds frustrating."

Use the Magic Mirror (Hack 1).

"I see the monster is telling you that forgetting your lunch is a catastrophe."

Then, offer a reality-based consequence or solution they must enact.

"It is noon now. I cannot drive to the school."

"You have two options."

"You can eat the school lunch."

"Or you can call Dad to see if he can drop something off after his meeting."

The point is they must now manage the consequences of the anxiety-induced mistake.

They learn they can survive the discomfort.

They learn they are competent problem solvers.

TRAP 3: NEGOTIATING WITH THE TERRORIST

Anxiety is a terrorist demanding ransom.

It says, "If you want to feel safe, you must wash your hands ten times."

Or, "If you want to go to the park, you must promise to stay within two feet of me."

When a parent negotiates, they give the monster leverage.

Negotiating sounds like this.

"Okay, you only have to wash your hands eight times, how about that."

"We can go to the park, but let's try to stay within five feet instead of two, is that a deal."

The parent is trying to meet the monster halfway.

They believe compromise will ease the transition.

But you cannot compromise with illogical fear.

You cannot reason with the monster.

When you negotiate, you are implicitly agreeing that the anxiety's demand has value.

The child learns that the rules are flexible.

They learn that if they argue and panic long enough, the requirement will drop.

To withdraw from the Negotiating Trap, use the Unflappable Anchor (Hack 3).

Your voice must be calm.

Your expectation must be unwavering.

You are the family leader.

You set the rules.

The rules are based on safety and logic, not the monster's whim.

If the expectation is washing hands once, it is washing hands once.

You validate their feeling.

"The monster sounds really upset about this."

Then you state the expectation.

"We wash our hands once in this house."

"We do not negotiate with fear."

Refuse to engage in the specific content of the anxiety.

Do not discuss the germs.

Discuss the boundary.

This shows confidence.

This shows leadership.

TRAP 4: REPETITIVE REASSURANCE AND SAFETY CHECKS

We covered this extensively in Hack 7.

But it warrants inclusion here because it is such a potent enabling trap.

Reassurance is a compulsion for the parent.

It relieves your stress in the moment.

It is like pouring water on a bonfire of worry.

The water turns to steam, making a dramatic show, but the fire is still burning underneath.

Your child asks, "Are we sure the smoke detector works."

You answer, "Yes, darling, I checked it yesterday, and we have a battery backup."

Temporary relief.

Ten minutes later, they ask again.

You answer, "I promise you, we are fine, go to sleep."

You just fed the fear.

Every time you give a direct, factual answer to an anxiety-driven question, you reinforce the need to check.

You are training your child to outsource their internal safety monitoring system to you.

The anxious brain says, "My internal radar is broken, I must rely on the external validator, which is Mom or Dad."

The only way to fix the radar is to refuse to check it for them.

To withdraw, you must utilize the scripted responses of Hack 7.

When they ask, "Are we safe."

You respond with a question.

"What does the monster want you to do."

"What do we know about how the anxiety works."

Or you use the confident script.

"We already talked about that."

"I am not going to answer that question, and that's a hard stop."

It feels cold at first.

It is not cold.

It is rehabilitation.

It is healing the child's brain by denying the compulsive checking behavior.

Trap 5: The Silent Family Sacrifice.

This trap happens slowly over months or years.

The anxiety starts small.

A fear of dogs.

Then, to keep the peace, the family simply stops going to the dog park.

Then, friends who own dogs are no longer invited over.

Then, the family starts driving an extra mile around the neighbourhood just to avoid seeing a dog walker.

The anxiety has colonized the entire family unit.

The family sacrifices joy, convenience, and normal activities to accommodate the monster.

Maybe your child has a severe fear of vomiting (emetophobia).

The entire family stops eating at restaurants.

They only eat bland, safe foods at home.

Maybe your child has separation anxiety at night.

So the co-parent is forced out of the marital bed to sleep elsewhere.

This is a massive enabling trap because it confirms to the child that their fear is powerful enough to dictate the lives of everyone around them.

It makes them the emotional center of the family system.

This power reinforces the anxiety cycle.

To withdraw from the Silent Family Sacrifice, you must institute Confident Boundary Setting (Hack 8).

You need to identify every way the family schedule, travel plans, or meal times have shifted due to the anxiety.

Make a list of the accommodations.

You are going to systematically reverse them.

This requires a family meeting.

You calmly explain that the household is under new management.

The anxiety monster is losing its voting rights.

Start with the easiest reversal.

If you stopped eating certain healthy foods due to a fear, put that food back on the menu tonight.

If you stopped listening to a certain kind of music in the car, put it back on.

If you are avoiding a specific grocery store because it triggers a worry, go there tomorrow.

Your confidence dictates the outcome here.

You do not ask the child's permission.

You announce the change with firm, loving authority.

"We are going back to the pre-anxiety normal."

This teaches the child that they can feel anxious and still move forward.

This teaches them that their fear is not the CEO of the family.

Your mission now is to become the Chief Withdrawal Officer.

Every time you feel the urge to rescue, accommodate, or reassure, stop.

Ask yourself one question.

Am I helping my child feel better right now, or am I helping my child get better long-term.

The difference between those two outcomes is the difference between enabling and empowerment.

You choose empowerment.

You choose long-term freedom.

You choose to be the coach.

Withdraw gracefully but resolutely from these traps.

Your child needs you to stop walking on eggshells.

They need you to hold the line.

They need you to show them that the world is worth stepping into, fear and all.

Start today.

Pick one trap you are currently caught in.

Reverse one small accommodation tonight.

This is how the living room takeback begins.

CHAPTER TEN

—★-★-★—

TROUBLESHOOTING: THE EMERGENCY TOOLKIT FOR CRISIS MOMENTS - STEP-BY-STEP INSTRUCTIONS FOR CRUSHING SCHOOL REFUSAL AND SEVERE SEPARATION ANXIETY WITHOUT SCREAMING

This chapter is your panic button.

It is the emergency toolkit.

You have learned the hacks.

Now you need to know exactly how to deploy them when the floor melts out from under you.

These moments are intense.

They are designed to make you feel powerless.

They are designed to make you scream or cave in.

We will not do either of those things.

We are maintaining firm, loving, absolute control.

Remember the Unflappable Anchor strategy.

You are the rock in the storm.

Your child needs to see you handle the crisis without dissolving into panic yourself.

This is the moment your confidence matters most.

CRISIS MOMENT 1: THE FULL-BLOWN PANIC ATTACK

A PANIC ATTACK IS A PHYSICAL EVENT.

It is not a character flaw.

It is a massive wave of adrenaline and fear chemistry.

The brain is convinced there is an immediate threat.

Your goal is not to talk them out of it.

Your goal is to safely ride the wave with them.

You must apply Hack 3: The Unflappable Anchor.

STEP 1: STOP THE NEGOTIATION

THE MOMENT THE PANIC STARTS, YOU STOP ALL OTHER ACTIVITIES.

You do not try to bargain.

You do not try to ask questions about the trigger.

The brain is offline for logical processing.

All talking stops.

STEP 2: COMMAND CALM PRESENCE

YOU MUST LOWER YOUR VOICE.

Slow your movements down dramatically.

Do not fuss over them.

Do not rush to get a glass of water or a paper bag.

This sends the message that the panic is a dire emergency requiring urgent action.

Instead, sit down next to them.

Make sure you are slightly elevated or at the same level.

Place your feet firmly on the ground.

Model physical stillness.

STEP 3: RADICAL VALIDATION WITHOUT REASSURANCE (HACK 1)

Use language that acknowledges the physical horror they are experiencing.

Say: Your heart is racing right now.

Say: I see your stomach is churning.

Say: This feels terrible and scary.

Do not say: You are fine.

Do not say: Nothing bad is happening.

You are validating the feeling, not the fear content.

STEP 4: REQUIRE STILLNESS AND TIME

The panic wants them to run, scream, or hide.

You must counter this urge.

If they are safe to do so, ask them to sit or lie down next to you.

Use a firm, quiet command.

Say: You need to stay still here with me until the adrenaline crests.

If they try to run away, gently block the exit path.

You are physically creating the containment field.

They must ride out the wave.

They must habituate to the physical feeling of fear (Hack 5).

The panic attack lasts 7 to 10 minutes, peak to resolution.

You are simply waiting out the clock, providing firm, silent company.

STEP 5: THE POST-PANIC TRANSITION

When the panic subsides, they will be exhausted.

The anxiety monster will immediately look for an accommodation (Hack 9).

It will say: I can't go to school now.

It will say: I need to stay home.

You must immediately deploy the Confident Boundary (Hack 8).

The event is over.

The plan is back on.

Say: That was awful, but you handled it.

Say: Now we are moving onto the next thing.

If the panic happened while driving to the library, you continue to the library.

Do not let the panic attack become an avoidance trophy.

—★–★–★—

CRISIS MOMENT 2: EXTREME SCHOOL REFUSAL

School refusal is a severe avoidance ritual.

It often presents with physical symptoms like nausea or stomach pain.

The child is not trying to be manipulative.

They are responding to overwhelming physiological terror.

However, you cannot treat the symptom.

You must treat the avoidance.

School is non-negotiable (Hack 8).

The goal is swift, unemotional movement toward the door.

STEP 1: PRE-EMPTIVE BLOCKING OF RITUALS (HACK 6)

The battle starts the night before.

Refuse all excessive reassurance questions about the next day.

If they start asking about the bus or the teacher, use a ritual blocking script.

Say: That is enough school talk for tonight.

Say: That is what the worry bully wants you to think about.

Move the conversation to a neutral topic immediately.

STEP 2: THE MORNING SCRIPT AND PACE

The morning must be fast, predictable, and devoid of emotional conversation.

You are a confident captain guiding a ship through rough seas.

Use Hack 2: The Language Reset.

If they say: My stomach hurts too much to eat.

Say: I know the anxiety monster makes your tummy hurt when it is worried about school.

Say: But we know that going to school is how we show the monster who is boss.

Then shift the focus back to the task.

Say: Put your shoes on now.

STEP 3: REFUSING ACCOMMODATIONS (HACK 9)

Do not allow stalling behaviours.

Do not let them negotiate for five more minutes.

Do not allow them to call the school nurse to ask about the day's activities.

These are all accommodations that feed the fear.

If they vomit, clean it up quickly and calmly.

The plan remains the same.

Say: I understand your body reacted to fear.

Say: Now we are putting your coat on.

STEP 4: THE FORCED TRANSITION (UNFLAPPABLE ANCHOR)

If the child physically refuses to move, clinging to you or the furniture, you must use your parental authority and size.

This must be done calmly and firmly, without anger or raised voices.

You are simply performing a necessary physical maneuver.

Say: It is time to go.

Gently and firmly take their hand or lift them.

Walk them to the car or the door.

If they thrash or scream, maintain a neutral expression.

You are modeling that their powerful emotions do not control your actions.

The fight response only works if you join it.

You refuse to join the fight.

STEP 5: THE DROP-OFF PROTOCOL (HACK 10)

The moment you arrive at school, the goodbye must be quick.

Do not linger.

Linger only reinforces the idea that something dangerous might happen after you leave.

Use the pre-agreed upon script.

Say: I love you.

Say: I know you can handle this hard thing.

Say: See you at 3 PM.

Then leave.

Do not look back.

Do not listen to the final plea for reassurance.

This requires incredible bravery from you.

It is the most powerful moment of exposure for your child.

You are teaching their brain that they survive the fear of separation.

CRISIS MOMENT 3: SEVERE SEPARATION ANXIETY

Separation anxiety at home often surfaces at night.

It is about control and certainty.

The anxiety troll demands that the parent is always visible or available.

This is where ritual blocking and boundary setting merge into an intense test.

STEP 1: DEFLECTING THE REASSURANCE SEEKERS (HACK 7)

Bedtime is often when the child attempts to extract endless reassurance.

They ask if you will check on them.

They ask if the door is locked.

They ask if you promise not to leave the house.

You must block these questions instantly.

Use a deflective script.

Say: That sounds like a question for the worry monster.

Say: We are done talking about those kinds of worries until morning.

Say: You already know the answer to that question.

Do not give the specific, comforting answer they are seeking.

Reassurance is poison.

STEP 2: ENFORCING THE SLEEP BOUNDARY (HACK 8)

The boundary is: You sleep in your bed.

When the child inevitably shows up at your door, often minutes after tuck-in, you must be a silent, powerful presence.

Do not engage in conversation.

Do not allow negotiation.

This is not a loving hug time.

This is a boundary enforcement moment.

STEP 3: THE SILENT RETURN (THE HABITUATION DRILL)

If they enter your room, stand up immediately.

Take their hand, or place a hand on their back.

Walk them back to their room.

Say absolutely nothing.

Use zero eye contact if possible.

This lack of reward (conversation, attention, comfort) makes the behavior inefficient for the anxiety.

You are a robot executing a program.

You are not angry.

You are not hostile.

You are just firm.

If they resist, hold the door open and wait for them to enter.

STEP 4: THE REPEATED DRILL

They may return ten times.

They may return twenty times.

The consistency of your silent return is the treatment.

Every time you take them back without talking, you are performing an exposure.

You are forcing them to habituate to the discomfort of being alone (Hack 5).

The anxiety levels spike, but when the parent remains an unflappable anchor, the spike eventually falls faster and stays lower.

The ritual of seeking comfort fails.

STEP 5: HANDLING THE PHYSICAL CLING

Sometimes the child will physically prevent you from leaving their room or refuse to let go of your leg.

You must use gentle, unyielding pressure to withdraw.

If you must, wait three minutes until the physical intensity subsides slightly.

Then, gently peel them away.

Say: I am leaving now.

Say: You are safe here.

Then leave swiftly.

Do not let the physical cling override the boundary.

The anxiety only wins if you stay in the room or allow them to stay in yours.

—★-★-★—

MASTERING THE CRISIS MOMENT

The common denominator in all three crises is confidence.

You must project absolute certainty in the plan.

The anxiety is loud.

Your certainty must be louder.

Remember that every time you implement a hack during a crisis, you are rewiring their brain in real-time.

You are teaching their nervous system a new truth.

The truth is: Fear happens.

The truth is: Mom/Dad stays steady.

The truth is: I survive the fear without escaping or getting reassurance.

Do not be afraid of their tears or their anger.

Anger is often a deflection of intense fear.

Your job is not to eliminate their distress instantly.

Your job is to contain their distress and enforce the plan.

You are the emergency toolkit.

You already have the pieces.

Use them now.

Be the anchor.

Do not sink with the ship.

CHAPTER ELEVEN

THE 7-DAY BATTLE PLAN: EXACTLY WHICH 3 HACKS TO DEPLOY STARTING MONDAY MORNING (AND HOW TO MEASURE $1,000 WORTH OF PROGRESS BY FRIDAY)

You have reached the activation point.

The time for reading theory is over.

The time for talking generally about anxiety is done.

Now we are moving into execution.

This chapter is the ultimate synthesis of everything you have learned.

We are not going to try to boil the ocean.

We are going to focus like a laser beam.

Starting Monday morning, you have a specific, measurable mission.

You will only deploy three of the ten powerful hacks you now possess.

These three hacks are chosen because they are 100 percent in your control.

You do not need your child's cooperation for success in Week One.

You only need your own commitment.

This plan will change the landscape of your living room dramatically.

You are going to measure progress not in how your child feels, but in how powerfully you respond.

This is the parent's transformation week.

The Core Three Hacks for Week 1.

We are establishing the new foundation.

We need new language.

We need bulletproof composure.

We need to stop the primary enabling behavior immediately.

Your Core Three Hacks are Hack 1, Hack 3, and Hack 7.

These are the non-negotiables.

Hack 1 is The Magic Mirror Validation Technique.

You learned to say, I see you are scared.

You learned to stop providing fake or real certainty.

This week, we implement the Language Reset Protocol fully.

Every single time your child expresses worry, you respond with validation of the feeling, but zero reassurance of the outcome.

The child might say, What if I get sick at school.

Your old response was, You will be fine, I packed you medicine, you are safe.

Your new Hack 1 response is, I see the worry monster is trying to make you scared about being sick.

That is a mean trick it plays.

But we do not let the monster decide.

We are going to school anyway.

Hack 1 establishes that you are aware of the fight.

It teaches your child that you are a teammate against the anxiety, not an enemy who dismisses their feelings.

It also starves the need for certainty.

Hack 3 is The Unflappable Anchor Strategy.

This is about your physical and emotional demeanor.

When a meltdown hits, your child is looking for a leader.

They are looking for a rock.

If you join their panic, the anxiety wins instantly.

Hack 3 demands that you model unwavering calm.

Your heart rate must stay steady.

Your voice must stay low and even.

You must not negotiate, yell, or plead.

You become the Anchor.

This week, you will practice the physical posture of calm leadership.

Shoulders back.

Breath slow.

Eyes steady.

You are the adult.

You are the confident coach.

You are practicing this demeanor whether you are scared or not.

Feelings follow actions.

Act like the Anchor, and soon you will feel like the Anchor.

Hack 7 is The Reassurance TRAP.

This is the biggest energy drain in an anxious household.

The child asks, Did you check the stove.

The child asks, Are you sure the door is locked.

The child asks, Will my friend still like me tomorrow.

The child asks, Is the food poisoned.

Every single answer you provide is a poison pill.

It gives immediate, temporary relief.

It guarantees the question will be asked again, louder, in five minutes.

Hack 7 is the immediate and complete cessation of all reassurance.

This means you must have your scripts ready.

When they ask for reassurance, you must deflect.

You must use a confident redirect.

You might say, That sounds like a job for your strong brain, not mine.

You might say, We already talked about that, but the worry monster does not like the answer.

You might say, I trust you to handle the uncertainty.

No matter what, do not engage with the content of the fear.

Hack 7 is the crucial step to stop fueling the entire system.

The 7-Day Deployment Timeline.

We start small and build momentum fast.

Commit right now to Monday through Friday deployment.

No matter what happens, you stick to the plan.

Monday is Language Day.

Your sole focus is Hack 1.

You will catch every single moment of worry talk.

You will replace your old reassuring responses with the Magic Mirror validation scripts.

You are focusing on separating the child from the monster.

Write down five scripts on a card and keep it in your pocket.

This is not about perfection.

This is about high repetition.

Your goal is 15 successful deployments of Hack 1 today.

Tuesday is Blockade Day.

You are deploying Hack 7.

The requests for reassurance will increase when you start Hack 1.

The anxiety bully is testing your new boundaries.

It senses weakness.

You must be ready for this test.

Every single request for certainty is met with a practiced, firm, loving deflection script.

Do not argue.

Do not explain the logic.

Do not apologize.

You are using a calm, boring voice for the deflective script.

Your goal is to deflect 100 percent of all reassurance requests today.

It will feel hard.

It will create friction.

That friction is the anxiety system fighting for its life.

That means you are winning.

Wednesday is Integration Day.

You are using Hack 1 and Hack 7 together perfectly.

The child is worried about a test.

You say, I see the monster making you scared about the test, Hack 1.

The child asks, Will I pass if I study for one more hour.

You say, You know exactly what you need to do, Hack 7.

You are a confident, coordinated machine today.

You are also focusing on zero accommodation.

If anxiety demands you drive a specific route, you drive a different route.

If anxiety demands you repeat the bedtime ritual, you stop halfway through.

Today is the day you visibly take back control.

Every time you say no to the monster, it is a massive victory.

Thursday is Anchor Day.

You are deploying Hack 3.

You have established a baseline of conflict with the anxiety bully.

The bully might escalate.

This is a good sign.

Anticipate the moment when a meltdown or panic is likely.

If it is drop-off, prepare your Anchor stance.

If it is homework time, prepare your Anchor stance.

Focus 100 percent on your body language.

Your goal is to remain perfectly calm for the entire duration of the panic event.

Do not engage with the fear content during the panic.

If they are screaming, simply stand close and say in a low voice, I am here.

I am the anchor.

We are safe.

Repeat that simple mantra internally and externally.

Your performance as the Anchor is the only metric that matters today.

Friday is Progress Measurement Day.

This is the synthesis of all three hacks.

Today you operate on all cylinders.

Use Hack 1 language constantly.

Block Hack 7 reassurance requests instantly.

Deploy Hack 3 whenever the system tries to override you.

We are now calculating the $1,000 worth of progress you have made.

How to Measure $1,000 Worth of Progress.

We are not measuring if the anxiety is gone.

That is a long-term goal.

We are measuring the return on your emotional investment.

We are measuring what you have reclaimed.

We assign a dollar value to every successful parental action.

This makes the progress visible and tangible.

Value of one successful Hack 1 deployment: $20.

You stopped a worry spiral before it began.

You reframed the narrative.

If you did this 50 times this week, that is $1,000 right there.

Value of one successful Hack 7 reassurance block: $50.

You broke the cycle of dependence.

You saved 20 minutes of repetitive questioning and escalating worry.

If you blocked 20 requests this week, that is another $1,000.

Value of one successful Hack 3 Anchor performance during a meltdown: $250.

You prevented an hour of emotional recovery time.

You gave your child a neurological pathway to calm.

You showed undeniable leadership.

If you did this four times this week, you are at $1,000 already.

The point of this financial metric is to shift your focus from your child's struggle to your own execution.

You are focusing on your behavior.

You are the variable that you can control.

Write down your victories.

Tally up your score.

If you successfully deployed all three hacks and hit $1,000 worth of measured action, you won Week One.

Your living room is starting to feel different.

You are starting to breathe differently.

Your child is starting to test the new boundaries, which is exactly what should happen.

Friction means movement.

Conflict means change.

The Path Forward.

You have the foundation now.

This focused week established your leadership.

It proved to the anxiety bully that a new sheriff is in town.

It proved to yourself that you are capable of the hard, firm, compassionate boundary setting required.

The most important thing you have learned this week is simple.

You are the solution.

You do not have to wait for a therapist's appointment.

You do not have to wait for medication.

You do not have to wait for your child to feel ready.

You are ready.

The plan is clear.

The hacks are deployed.

Go be the leader your family needs and deserves.

You have everything required to guarantee success now.

Start Monday.

I believe in your strength.

I believe in your commitment.

Go take back your living room.

AFTERWORD

THE FINAL WORD: THE ONE CONFIDENCE SWITCH YOU MUST FLIP TODAY TO GUARANTEE SUCCESS

You made it.

You finished the book.

You absorbed the knowledge.

Now comes the critical part.

Now you must act.

Remember how you felt on page one.

That heavy burden of exhaustion.

That persistent, gnawing feeling of failing your child.

That feeling is not your truth anymore.

That feeling is gone.

We are flipping a switch right now.

Replace that old exhaustion with a focused, sharp purpose.

You are equipped.

You have 10 powerful tools in your arsenal.

These are not vague strategies.

These are science-backed protocols for dismantling anxiety.

You know the mechanism of fear now.

You understand the exact steps to interrupt the cycle.

But there is one switch that governs the success of all the other ten.

It is the only confidence switch that guarantees a positive outcome.

It is your confidence.

Your child is constantly looking to you for data.

When they are scared, they check your face.

When they feel the anxiety tightening its grip, they gauge your reaction.

If they see panic or accommodation in your eyes, they internalize that fear as legitimate and overwhelming.

They learn that the world is indeed dangerous.

The one switch you must flip today is the realization that you are the Anchor.

You are the steady force.

Your inner belief in the plan must be unwavering.

You must project absolute, calm certainty that the anxiety monster is a nuisance, not a threat.

Your child is looking for their leader.

Show them that the leader is calm.

Show them that the leader is in control.

You are no longer reacting to symptoms.

You are now strategically deploying treatment.

That is the difference between helplessness and power.

You have earned this competence.

Go back to your living room.

Stop walking on those eggshells.

Stop enabling the fear monster's demands.

You have the power to dismantle this cycle, starting today.

You know the scripts.

You know the boundaries.

You know how to validate the feeling without fuelling the fear.

Go be the firm coach your child desperately needs.

Go be the loving parent who holds the line.

Go be the powerful force that brings lasting freedom.

I believe in you.

www.ingramcontent.com/pod-product-compliance
Lightning Source LLC
LaVergne TN
LVHW050922210926
848482LV00012B/494

* 9 7 9 8 2 9 5 5 3 7 2 9 5 *